# HOW GOD DECORATES HEAVEN for CHRISTMAS

## RON MEHL AND MELODY CARLSON

ILLUSTRATED BY LYNN BREDESON

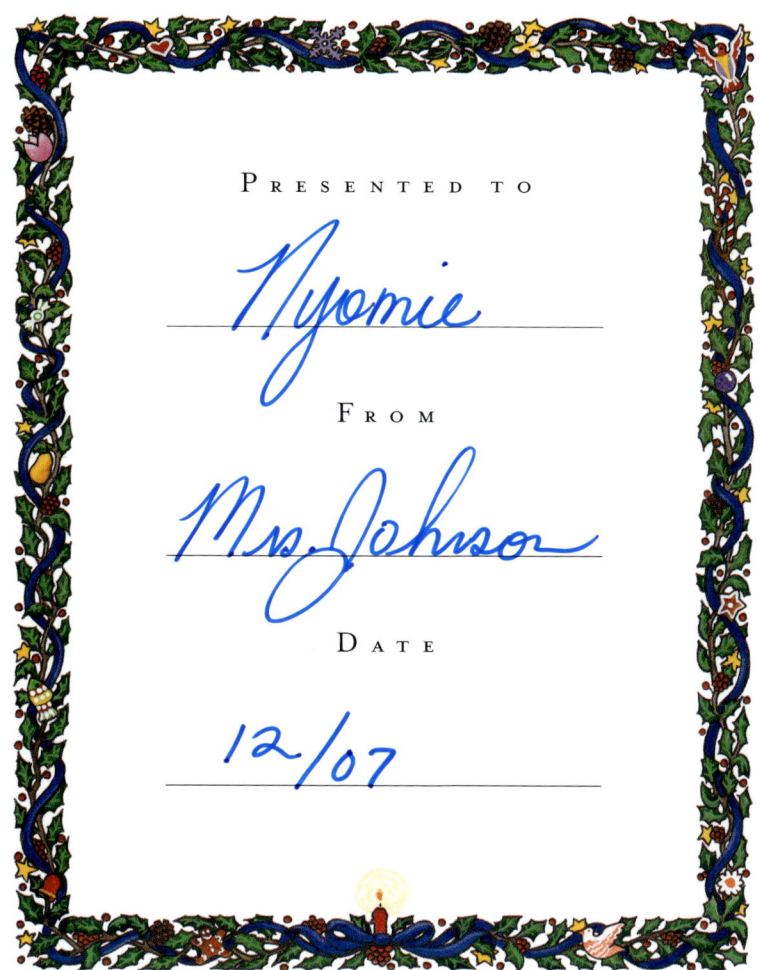

How God Decorates Heaven *for* Christmas

That very first Christmas,

One black, silent night,

God lit the whole sky

With a star burning bright.

And down in a manger

In a stable forlorn,

God poured out His love

When Jesus was born.

How God Decorates Heaven *for* Christmas

God woke up the shepherds,

And angels did sing

Sweet praises of gladness

To greet the new King!

With angels and starshine

The Lord decorated.

That's how His Son's birth

Was first celebrated.

HOW GOD DECORATES HEAVEN *for* CHRISTMAS

Now many years later,

We want it done right.

But how can we do it

Like on that first night?

We get out the tinsel.

We put up our tree.

We light up our lights

For our neighbors to see.

How God Decorates Heaven *for* Christmas

But sometimes I wonder,

Does God celebrate?

For Christmas in heaven,

Does He decorate?


Does God get out tinsel?

Does He get a tree?

Does He light up lights

For all heaven to see?

How God Decorates Heaven *for* Christmas

Does God trim His tree

With ribbons of rainbow,

Then swirl it with clouds

And splashes of moonglow?

How God Decorates Heaven *for* Christmas

Do angels spin silver

To flow like a fountain?

Do they gather up gold

In a shimmering mountain?

How God Decorates Heaven *for* Christmas

And do they weave garlands

Of twinkling starlight

To drape about heaven?

A glorious sight!

HOW GOD DECORATES HEAVEN *for* CHRISTMAS

Do angels thread diamonds

On long, sparkly strings

With rubies and emeralds

While all heaven sings?

How God Decorates Heaven *for* Christmas

Do they make ornaments

Like birds, bells, and flowers,

Then paint them with stardust?

Why, that must take hours!

How God Decorates Heaven *for* Christmas

Christmas in heaven

Must be oh, so grand!

Each star hangs in place,

So perfectly planned.

How God Decorates Heaven *for* Christmas

But something is missing

And something's not right,

Unless we remember

That first silent night.

When angels and shepherds

Did worship the One

Who came down from heaven,

God's very own Son.

How God Decorates Heaven *for* Christmas

When Jesus was born,

That was only the start—

The reason He came

Is to live in your heart!

Place child's photo above.

HOW GOD DECORATES HEAVEN *for* CHRISTMAS

*N*ow Christmas in heaven

Will be splendid, too.

God's best decoration

In heaven is YOU!

Dear boys and girls,

    Don't you love Christmas decorations? I do! They make me think of wonderful things:

- ✶ Sparkling lights remind me that Jesus is the light of the world.
- ✶ Beautiful presents with colorful bows remind me that Jesus is the greatest gift of all.
- ✶ The Christmas tree reminds me that Jesus died on a wooden cross to show you and me how much He loves us.

    So why would God decorate heaven for Christmas? I think it's because He must love Christmas, too. After all, it's the birthday of His Son!

    If you haven't received the gift of Jesus into your heart, I hope you'll make that decision today. Just pray, "Dear God, I want to accept Jesus as my Savior," and He'll come into your heart and forgive you of all your sins. You'll find Jesus to be the most special gift you've ever received. And then you, too, can be one of God's best decorations in heaven.

From my heart to yours, Merry Christmas!

*Ron Mehl*

DR. RON MEHL is a beloved pastor and award-winning author. His books include *God Works the Night Shift*, *The Tender Commandments*, and *A Prayer That Moves Heaven*. Ron and his wife, Joyce, have two married sons and two grandchildren and live in Oregon.

MELODY CARLSON is an award-winning author of more than sixty-five books for teens, women, and children. She enjoys an active lifestyle of hiking, skiing, and boating in the beautiful Oregon Cascade Mountains with her husband, two sons, and a prized Labrador retriever.

LYNN BREDESON is an artist and illustrator who enjoys painting the moments in time that the Lord gives as gifts to His children. She lives in Bend, Oregon, with her husband, two children, and one spoiled papillon dog.

How God Decorates Heaven for Christmas

published by Multnomah Publishers, Inc.

© 2003 by Ronald D. Mehl, Trustee
and Melody Carlson

International Standard Book Number: 1-59052-245-1

Cover art by Lynn Bredeson

*Multnomah* is a trademark of Multnomah Publishers, Inc.,
and is registered in the U.S. Patent and Trademark Office.
The colophon is a trademark of Multnomah Publishers, Inc.

Printed in South Korea

ALL RIGHTS RESERVED

No part of this publication may be reproduced, stored in a retrieval system,
or transmitted, in any form or by any means—electronic, mechanical,
photocopying, recording, or otherwise—without prior written permission.

For information:
MULTNOMAH PUBLISHERS, INC.
POST OFFICE BOX 1720
SISTERS, OREGON 97759

03 04 05 06 07 08—10 9 8 7 6 5 4 3 2 1